ISBN:
978-81-7436-722-8

VL.2

Hors d'oeuvres

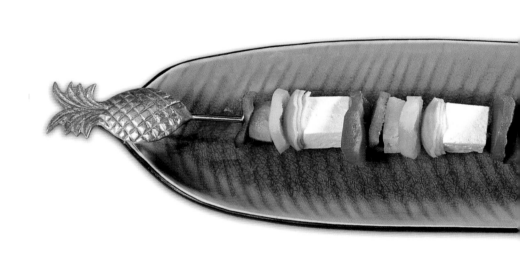

Hors d'oeuvres

EASY PARTY FOOD

Lustre Press
Roli Books

Contents

Introduction

Just as a well-stocked bar and irresistible cocktails enable a swinging start to a party, a tempting variety of snacks will sustain your guests throughout the party. Alcohol with insufficient food is a classic mistake to avoid, so plan an extensive snack menu.

Pre-party work is essential, as you want to relax and enjoy the occasion with your guests. Make sure you have enough serving bowls, platters, crockery, glasses, paper napkins, table covers and other practical items required for the party.

Canapés and savouries are perfect for serving with drinks before dinner but if you plan a longer party, be sure to provide a steady supply of snacks. The sensible option for larger parties is to provide a variety of nibbles, and to make a selection of home-made savouries and snacks as the main focus for the party. Hot snacks are also appreciated. This book gives you an array of 29 timeless favourites – from onion dip, buttered nuts to easy-to-make kebabs and spring rolls.

Presentation is important – the food should look as good as it tastes. A few tips to get you started:

Fresh is best – keep the food fresh by making sure you have plenty of refrigerator space to keep items chilled before they are served.

Neat arrangements – snacks, savouries and canapés should be neatly arranged on platters and topped up as necessary.

Distribute evenly – it is better to divide the snacks into several portions and place them evenly throughout the room.

For a successful party, the host must balance relaxation with energy – being at ease with your role will make your friends feel at home. A delectable display of snacks helps in creating an impression and can be used to introduce and mix groups of guests, lightening heavy conversation, making sure everyone has someone to talk to, and even, rescuing those who are cornered by others from whom they would prefer to escape!

Most importantly, remember to enjoy the party!

Onion Dip

Ingredients:

30 gm / 1 oz / ¼ Stick butter

1 tbsp Olive oil

2 Large onions, very finely chopped

2 Thyme sprigs

1 Bay leaf

½ tsp Sugar

125 g / 4 oz / 1 cup Mature (sharp)
Cheddar cheese, finely grated

4 tbsp Mayonnaise

6 tbsp Greek yoghurt, fromage frais or
whipped cream

2 tbsp Parsley finely chopped

Salt and freshly ground black pepper

To dip:

Tortilla chips, Potato crisps, Breadsticks,
Carrot sticks, Celery sticks, Radishes

Method:

Melt the butter with the oil in a small saucepan. Add the onions, thyme and bay. Stir well, cover the pan and cook for 15 minutes. Remove the lid and stir in the sugar. Continue to cook, stirring often, for a further 15-20 minutes, until the onions are very soft and creamy and lightly browned. Remove from the heat and discard the herbs. Spoon into a bowl and allow to cool.

Add the cheese to the onions and pound together until thoroughly combined. Stir in the mayonnaise, yoghurt, parsley, salt and pepper to taste. Chill lightly before serving with the suggested ingredients to dip.

Crunchy Hummus

Ingredients:

2 Coriander seeds, coarsely ground

1 tbsp Dill seeds

1 tbsp Celery seeds

1 Slice of onion

1 Garlic clove

2 tbsp Tahini

439 gm / 15 oz can Chickpeas (garbanzo beans), drained

200 ml / 7 fl oz / scant 1 cup Peanut oil

Salt and freshly ground black pepper

To dip:

Mini pita breads, Rice cakes, Carrot sticks, Green pepper (capsicum, bell pepper) sticks

Method:

Roast the coriander, dill and celery seeds in a dry, heavy-bottomed saucepan until lightly browned and aromatic; do not overcook them or they will taste bitter. Grind the seeds in a mortar, using a pestle. Then put into a food processor or blender with the onion and garlic, and process to a coarse paste.

Add the tahini and continue processing the mixture to grind any remaining whole seeds. Add the chickpeas in two batches, processing coarsely; then slowly trickle in the oil with the machine running. The mixture will form a creamy paste. Add the lemon juice, with salt and pepper to taste and process briefly. Serve with the suggested ingredients to dip.

Ricotta and Sun-dried Tomato Dip

Ingredients:

6 Sun-dried tomatoes

2 Olive oil

4 Red wine

1 Garlic clove, finely chopped

225g / 8 oz / 1 cup Ricotta cheese

125 gm/4 oz/scant ½ cup Mascarpone cheese

1 Spring onion (scallion), finely chopped

6 Large Basil leaves, finely shredded

Salt and freshly ground black pepper

Method:

This is delicious with breadsticks, tiny crackers or Melba toasts. Chop the sun-dried tomatoes or snip them into small pieces with a pair of scissors. Put into a small saucepan with the olive oil, red wine and chopped garlic clove. Heat slowly, stirring, until boiling, then cover the pan and cook gently for 15 minutes. Remove the lid and boil until the liquid has evaporated, leaving the tomatoes moist and tender. Set aside to cool.

Press the Ricotta cheese through a fine sieve (strainer); then mix in the mascarpone cheese, spring onion (scallion), tomatoes and their juices, Basil leaves and salt and pepper to taste. Chill for at least an hour to allow the flavours to develop before serving.

Taramasalata

Ingredients:

1 Medium slice of white bread, crusts removed

4 tbsp Water

225 g/8 oz Smoked cod's roe, skinned

1 Garlic clove

1 Thin slice of onion, finely chopped

2 tbsp Lemon juice

150 ml / ¼ print / ⅔ cup Olive oil

Freshly ground black pepper

To dip:

Mini pita breads

Pitted black (ripe) olives

Melba toasts

Assorted crudités

Method:

Put the bread into a bowl and sprinkle the water over it. Set aside for 15 minutes; then squeeze the water from the bread. Put the roe in a food processor or blender with the bread, garlic and onion. Add 1 tablespoon of the lemon juice and 2 tablespoons of the olive oil. Process until smooth; then gradually trickle in the remaining oil while the machine is working. The mixture will form a creamy, mayonnaise-like mixture.

Season to taste with pepper and the remaining lemon juice. Chill lightly and serve with a selection of ingredients to dip.

Por Pia Savoey
Thai Spring Rolls

Ingredients:

120 gm Vermicelli, soaked for 10 minutes

120 gm Cabbage, shredded

60 gm Carrots, shredded

40 gm Spring onions, shredded

60 gm Onions, shredded

4 tbsp / 60 ml Oil

Salt to taste Pepper to taste

2 tsp / 10 ml Soy sauce

16 Spring roll skins

½ cup / 100 ml Plum sauce

Method:

Heat 1 tbsp oil in a pan; add the vegetables and sauté for a few minutes.

Add the vermicelli, salt and pepper to taste and the soy sauce. Sauté further for a few seconds.

Remove from the heat and place on a perforated vessel to allow it to cool. Divide the mixture into 4 equal portions.

Roll the portions into the spring roll skins and deep-fry in hot oil. Remove and keep aside.

Serve hot, accompanied by plum sauce.

Satay Kai
Satay Sticks

Ingredients:

600 gm Chicken, boneless

8 tsp / 40 gm Curry powder

3 tbsp / 45 gm Garlic cloves

8 tsp / 40 gm Coriander root

1 tbsp / 15 gm Coriander seeds

4 tsp / 20 gm White pepper powder

½ cup / 100 ml Fish sauce

8 tsp / 40 gm Lemon grass, chopped

5 tsp / 25 gm Galangal or kha chopped

4 tsp / 20 gm Cumin seeds

½ cup / 100 ml Peanut sauce

Method:

Cut the chicken into 2" broad strips.
Make a paste by mixing together the curry
powder, garlic cloves, coriander root,
coriander seeds, white pepper powder, fish
sauce, lemon grass, kha and cumin seeds.
Marinate the chicken strips in the prepared
paste for 4 hours.

Skewer the chicken strips on bamboo
sticks and grill / roast till the chicken is
done.

Remove from the heat and serve hot, on
the sticks themselves, accompanied by
peanut sauce.

Thord Man Koong
Grand Fish Mixed with Thai Spices

Ingredients:

400 gm Prawns, shelled, cleaned

80 gm Pork fat

4 tbsp / 60 ml Fish sauce

4 tsp / 20 ml Chinese wine

2 tsp / 10 gm White pepper powder

4 tsp / 20 gm Cornflour

4 tsp / 20 ml Sesame oil

4 tsp / 20 ml Light soy sauce

1 cup / 200 gm Breadcrumbs

Oil for frying

Method:

Mince the prawns and pork fat together. To the prawn mixture, add the fish sauce, Chinese wine, white pepper powder, cornflour, sesame oil, soy sauce and mix well.

Shape the mixture into small round cutlets. Coat with breadcrumbs and deep-fry in hot oil until golden brown in colour. Remove, drain the excess oil and place neatly on a serving platter.

Serve hot, accompanied by Nam Jim Buey sauce.

Deep-fried Prawn Dumpling

Ingredients:

10 Wonton skin

80 gm Prawns, cleaned, chopped

½ Egg, whisked

Salt to taste

½ tsp / 3 ml Chinese wine

½ tsp / 3 ml Sesame oil

20 gm Spring onions, chopped

Oil for frying

Method:

Mix the prawns along with the salt, egg, Chinese wine, sesame oil and spring onions. Divide the prawn mixture into 10 equal portions.

Place one portion of the filling in the centre of one wonton skin and fold to seal.

Repeat the same process with the remaining prawn mixture and wonton skins.

Heat the oil in a wok and deep-fry the prawn dumplings a few at a time.

Remove, drain the excess oil and serve hot.

23

Sesame Prawn Toast

Ingredients:

500 gm Prawns, cleaned

10 gm Ginger, julienned

1 tsp / 5 gm Salt

1 tsp / 5 ml Sesame oil

1 tsp / 5 ml Chinese wine

1 tsp / 5 gm Ajinomoto

2 Eggs, whisked

8 Bread slices

1 tbsp / 15 gm Sesame seeds, broiled

Oil for frying

Method:

Blend the prawns along with the ginger, salt, sesame oil, Chinese wine, ajinomoto and eggs.

Divide the mixture into 4 equal portions and spread each portion over the bread slices evenly.

Sprinkle the sesame seeds on top and keep aside.

Heat the oil in a wok and deep-fry the slices one by one till crisp on both sides.

Drain the excess oil and serve immediately, accompanied by sweet and sour sauce.

Steamed Prawns with Ginger

26

Ingredients:

500 gm Prawns, shelled

1 tsp / 5 gm Salt

1½ tsp / 8 gm Ajinomoto

2 Eggs, whisked

4 tsp / 20 gm Ginger, julienned

2 tsp / 10 ml Chinese wine

10 gm Green coriander, chopped

Method:

Arrange the prawns neatly in a pan; add the salt, ajinomoto, eggs and ginger. Mix well.

Cover the pan and steam the prawns for 10 minutes.

Remove from the heat; transfer into a serving bowl and pour the Chinese wine on top.

Serve immediately, garnished with green coriander.

Stuffed Potatoes

Ingredients:

10 Potatoes, large

For the filling:

60 gm Potatoes, cubed

60 gm Raisins

60 gm Cashew nuts, broken

60 gm Khoya

60 gm Almonds, slivered

For the marinade:

100 gm Yoghurt, hung

10 gm Garlic paste

10 gm Ginger paste

5 gm / 1 tsp Green chillies, minced

5 gm / 1 tsp Garam masala

Salt to taste

200 ml / 1 cup Oil (for basting)

45 gm Almonds, roasted

Method:

Cut the potatoes into barrels and scoop the inside out.

For the filling, mix together all the ingredients and stuff the hollow potatoes with it.

For the marinade, mix together all the ingredients and marinate the potatoes in it. Keep aside for 1½ hours.

Skewer the potatoes and cook in a tandoor for 15-20 minutes. Remove from tandoor, baste with oil and cook again for 5 minutes.

Remove from skewers and serve hot, garnished with roasted almonds.

Mint Cottage Cheese Cubes

Ingredients:

800 gm Cottage cheese

Salt to taste

5 gm / 1 tsp Red chilli powder

5 gm / 1 tsp Turmeric powder

5 Lemons

5 gm / 1 tsp Chaat masala

10 gm / 2 tsp Garam masala

75 gm Mint leaves, chopped

75 gm Green coriander, chopped

75 gm Ginger, chopped

25 gm Green chillies, chopped

250 gm Yoghurt

60 gm Ginger-garlic paste

25 gm / 5 tsp Yellow chilli powder

10 gm / 2 tsp Carom seeds

60 gm Butter

5 gm / 1 tsp White pepper powder

Method:

Cut the cottage cheese into equal sized cubes. Sprinkle salt to taste, red chilli powder and turmeric powder evenly on the cubes and keep aside.

Add lemon juice, half of chaat masala and garam masala, mix well.

Slit the cottage cheese cubes and fill with the chopped mint, coriander and green chillies.

Whisk yoghurt along with the remaining ingredients and coat the cubes evenly with this mixture.

Skewer the cubes and cook on a charcoal grill till completely done.

Remove from skewers, sprinkle the remaining chaat masala and garam masala on top and serve.

Cottage Cheese and Sago Kebab

Ingredients:

500 gm Cottage cheese

100 gm Sago

100 gm Spring onions, minced

10 gm Green chillies, chopped

45 gm Cashew nuts, broken

60 gm Raisins

5 gm / 1 tsp Cumin seeds, roasted

3 gm / ½ tsp Turmeric powder

5 gm / 1 tsp Garam masala

30 gm Cornflour

Salt to taste

Oil for frying

Method:

Mash the cottage cheese and heat it so that it leaves water. Squeeze and mash again.

Boil sago pellets and drain. Blend to break into smaller lumps without making it into a paste.

Mix together all the ingredients along with mashed cottage cheese and sago paste and knead. Keep aside for 30 minutes.

Shape into flat round cutlets. Heat a griddle, brush with oil and fry the cutlets a few at a time until golden brown in colour.

Remove, drain excess oil and serve hot.

Stuffed Green Pepper

Ingredients:

600 gm Capsicum

60 ml / 3½ tbsp Oil

15 gm Ginger, chopped

10 gm / 2 tsp Cumin seeds

100 gm Potatoes, boiled, diced

100 gm Cottage cheese

10 gm / 2 tsp Turmeric powder

5 gm / 1 tsp Garam masala

45 gm Cashew nuts

25 gm Raisins

15 gm Green chillies, chopped

15 gm Green coriander, chopped

Salt to taste

For the marinade:

200 gm Yoghurt, hung

20 gm Red chilli paste

20 gm Ginger-garlic paste

3 gm / ½ tsp Garam masala

Salt to taste

Butter for basting

3 gm / ½ tsp Cumin powder

Method:

Remove top of capsicums and scoop out seeds. Keep top aside.

Heat oil in a wok, add ginger and cumin seeds, sauté till they crackle, add potatoes and cottage cheese. Sauté for a few minutes. Stir in dry spices along with the remaining ingredients. Mix well and remove from heat.

Fill the capsicums with this mixture and cover with top. For the marinade, mix all the ingredients and coat the capsicums with it.

Skewer the capsicums and cook in a grill for 10 minutes. Remove, baste with butter and cook further for 2-5 minutes. Serve hot.

Murg Makhmali Kebab
Buttery Chicken Kebab

Ingredients:

800 gm Chicken breast fillets

100 gm Ginger-garlic paste

Salt to taste

200 gm Cream

100 gm Processed cheese

5 gm / 1 tsp White pepper powder

20 gm Green coriander, finely chopped

20 gm Green chillies, finely chopped

3 gm / ½ tsp Mace powder

3 gm / ½ tsp Nutmeg powder

3 Eggs, white

60 gm Butter

Method:

Clean the chicken fillets, rub ginger-garlic paste and salt evenly on them and keep aside.

Mix cream along with processed cheese, white pepper powder, green coriander, green chillies, mace and nutmeg powder and egg white. Coat the fillets evenly with this mixture. Keep aside for 2 hours.

Skewer the chicken fillets and roast in a moderately hot tandoor for 8-10 minutes, remove, baste with butter and roast again for 3-5 minutes.

Remove from skewers and serve hot.

Sarson ka Tikka
Mustard Flavoured, Roasted Chicken Tikka

Ingredients:

900 gm Chicken leg, boneless,
cut into pieces

100 ml / ½ tsp Lemon juice

Salt to taste

60 gm Ginger-garlic paste

100 gm Green coriander, chopped

75 gm Garlic, chopped

45 gm Green chillies, chopped

15 gm Yellow chilli paste

45 gm Mustard paste

120 ml / ½ cup Mustard oil

60 gm Gramflour

10 gm / 2 tsp Garam masala

60 gm Butter

Method:

Apply lemon juice, salt to taste and ginger-garlic paste evenly on the chicken pieces.

Make a paste by blending together green coriander, garlic and green chillies. To this add all the other ingredients except butter.

Squeeze the chicken pieces and add to the prepared paste. Mix well and keep aside for 3 to 4 hours.

Skewer the chicken pieces and cook in a tandoor or a charcoal grill for 10 minutes.

Remove from the tandoor, baste with butter and cook further until done.

Remove from skewers and serve hot.

Badam Ke Shammi Kebab
Almond and Lamb Mince Kebab

Ingredients:

1 kg / 2.2 lb Lamb, minced

30 gm / 1 oz Bengal gram

5 Dry red chillies

5 Green chillies, whole

5 Black cardamom

5 Bay leaves

5 Cinnamon, 1" sticks

10 Cloves

8 cups / 2 lt / 64 fl oz Water

3 Eggs

2 tsp / 4 gm Salt

½ cup / 60 gm / 2 oz Almonds, slivered

Vegetable oil for frying

Method:

Boil the minced lamb with Bengal gram, dry red chillies, green chillies, and all the whole spices till the water evaporates.

Remove and discard all the whole spices from the mixture. Mash the mince well.

Add eggs and salt and knead well. Mix in the almonds.

Divide the mixture into even-sized balls and shape into cutlets.

Heat the oil in a wok; deep-fry the cutlets until crisp and brown on all sides.

Remove and drain the excess oil on absorbent kitchen towels; serve hot.

Kebab-e-Chaman
Vegetarian Kebab

Ingredients:

1 kg Spinach

400 gm Potatoes

150 gm Lentils

25 gm Green chillies

25 gm Ginger

25 gm Green coriander

100 gm Raisins, finely chopped

20 gm / 4 tsp Cumin powder

15 gm / 1 tbs Coriander powder

10 gm / 2 tsp Dry fenugreek powder

100 gm Cashewnut, finely chopped

Salt to taste

150 gm Clarified butter

Methods:

Boil the spinach, potatoes and lentils separately.

Chop the spinach finely, mash the potatoes and lentils.

Chop green chillies, ginger and green coriander finely and mix into the mashed potatoes and lentils along with spinach and all the other ingredients except clarified butter.

Shape into flat round cutlets.

Heat a griddle and shallow fry the cutlets in clarified butter until crisp and golden brown on both sides.

Remove, drain excess clarified butter and serve hot.

Machhi Kohiwada
Deep-fried Batter Coated Fish Fillets

Ingredients:

500 gm / 1.1 lb Fish, betki fillets

2 tbsp / 30 ml / 1 fl oz Lemon juice

Salt to taste

½ tsp / 1 gm White pepper powder

½ cup Ginger-garlic paste

1 cup / 100 gm / 3½ oz Gram flour

2 tsp / 3 gm Cumin powder

2 tsp / 4 gm Chaat masala

1 tsp / 2 gm Garam masala

2 tbsp / 30 gm / 1 oz Red chilli paste

2 tsp Green chillies, chopped

2 tsp / 12 gm Ginger, chopped

½ cup / 60 gm / 2 oz Onions, chopped

1¼ cups / 250 ml / 8 fl oz Vegetable oil

Water as required

Method:

Cut the fish fillets into fish fingers and marinate with lemon juice, salt, white pepper powder, and ginger-garlic paste. Keep aside for 20 minutes.

In a bowl, mix all the other ingredients except the last two. Gradually add water to make a batter of coating consistency.

Heat the oil in a wok; dip the marinated fish fingers in the batter and deep-fry until crisp and golden brown.

Remove, drain the excess oil on absorbent kitchen towels and serve hot.

Pakora
Fritters

Ingredients:

1 Potato, large, peeled, sliced

1 Aubergine, small, sliced

1 Onion, large, sliced

For the Batter:

2 cups / 200 gm / 7 oz Gram flour

1 tsp / 4 gm Salt

1 tsp / 2 gm Red chilli powder

½ tsp / 3 gm Baking powder

Vegetable oil for frying

Method:

In a bowl, combine all the ingredients for the batter. Mix well, adding a little water to make a very thick batter.

Heat the oil in a wok; dip the sliced vegetables into the batter, one at a time, and deep-fry until crisp and golden brown. Remove with a slotted spoon and drain the excess oil on absorbent kitchen towels.

Serve hot with tomato sauce.

Pão com Chouriço
Goan Sausage

Ingredients:

1¼ cups / 200 gm / 7 oz Goa sausage
meat (chouriço)

1 Onion, large, thickly sliced

Vinegar to taste

Salt to taste

8 Small loaves of bread

Method:

Slit the casing of the sausages, and remove the meat. Cook in a pan with 1 cup water for 15 minutes or till the meat is cooked and the mixture is dry. Drain the excess fat.

Add the onion and cook for 3 minutes more, stirring occasionally. Adjust seasoning and add vinegar and salt if necessary.

Slit the loaves and fill with the sausage meat. Serve at once.

Fofos de Peixe
Fish Cakes

48

Ingredients:

500 gm / 1.1 lb Fish, (pomfret / seer / salmon), boneless, washed

½ tsp / 1 gm Turmeric powder

2 / 200 gm / 7 oz Potatoes, medium-sized, boiled, mashed

2 Onions, medium-sized, minced

1 tsp / 1″ piece Ginger, minced

1 tsp / 6 cloves Garlic, minced

2-3 Green chillies, minced

2 tbsp / 8 gm Green coriander, finely chopped

1½ -2 tbsp / 20-30 ml Lemon juice

Salt to taste

¼ tsp Black pepper powder

2 Eggs, beaten

1 cup approx. Breadcrumbs / Semolina

Vegetable oil for shallow frying

Method:

Steam the fish with ½ tsp salt, turmeric powder, and ½ cup water for 5-7 minutes. Drain and mash well, removing skin and bones if any.

Add the remaining ingredients, except breadcrumbs / semolina and oil. Mix well. Adjust seasoning.

On a flat surface, shape small quantities of the mixture into flat round / oval cakes or oblong croquettes. Roll in breadcrumbs / semolina and shallow fry the cakes / croquettes till golden. Serve hot with a spicy tomato sauce.

Crispy Sesame Prawns

Ingredients:

1 kg / 2.2 lb King prawns, shelled, deveined
Vegetable oil for frying

For the first marinade:
4 tsp / 24 gm Ginger paste
5 tsp / 30 gm / 1 oz Garlic paste
1 tsp / 2 gm Red chilli powder
1 tsp / 5 ml Lemon juice

For the second marinade:
4 tbsp / 60 gm / 2 fl oz Cheddar cheese, grated
1 tbsp Carom seeds
4 tbsp / 60 ml / 2 fl oz Cream
½ tsp / 1 gm Green cardamom powder
½ tsp / 1 gm Mace powder
3 tbsp / 30 gm / 1 oz Gram flour, roasted
½ cup / 100 gm / 3½ oz Yoghurt, drained
¼ cup Sesame seeds
½ cup / 60 gm / 2 oz Breadcrumbs

Method:

Mix all the ingredients of the first marinade and rub into the prawns. Keep aside for half an hour. Squeeze the prawns gently to remove the excess moisture.

Whisk together the ingredients for the second marinade (except sesame seeds and breadcrumbs) and marinate the prawns in this mixture for another 30 minutes.

Make a mixture of breadcrumbs and sesame seeds. Coat the prawns with the mixture and refrigerate for 15-20 minutes.

Heat the oil in a wok till it starts smoking. Lower heat and fry the prawns for 1-2 minutes. Remove, drain and keep aside for 4-5 minutes. Deep-fry again till they are crisp and golden in colour. Remove and drain the excess oil and serve hot.

Vegetable Samosa

Ingredients:
250 gm / 9 oz Refined flour
½ cup / 100 gm / 3½ oz Ghee
½ tsp / 1 gm Carom seeds
½ tsp / 2 gm Salt

For the filling:
3 tbsp / 45 ml / 1½ fl oz Vegetable oil
½ tsp / 1 gm Cumin seeds
250 gm / 9 oz Potatoes, boiled, finely diced
50 gm / 1¾ oz Green peas, boiled
½ tsp / 2 gm Salt
1 tsp / 1½ gm Coriander powder
½ tsp / 1 gm Turmeric powder
10 Green chillies, deseeded, finely chopped
Vegetable oil for frying

Method:
Mix ghee with flour and rub with your
fingertips till the mixture is crumbly. Add
carom seeds and salt. Mix well. Add just
a little water to make a firm but pliable
dough. Cover the dough with a moist cloth
and keep aside for half an hour.

Heat the oil in a wok; add cumin seeds.
When they crackle, add potatoes and green
peas. Stir for a minute. Add salt, coriander
powder, turmeric powder and green chillies.
Mix well and cook till the vegetables are
done. Keep the filling aside to cool.

Divide the dough equally into lemon-sized
balls. Flatten each ball and roll out to make a
thin 3" disc. Put a spoonful of the filling in half
of the disc. Fold the other half over enclosing
the filling, pressing the edges firmly to seal.

Heat the vegetable oil in a wok; deep-fry
the patties until golden brown. Remove and
drain on absorbent kitchen towels. Serve hot.

Spicy Meatballs

Ingredients:

550 gm / 16 oz / 3 cups Minced steak, lamb, pork, turkey or chicken

125 gm / 4 oz / ¼ cup Rindless bacon rashers (slices), finely chopped

1 large Onion, grated

2 Green chillies deseeded and chopped

2 tbsp Tomato paste

2 tbsp Whole-grain mustard

½ tsp Ground mace

Salt and freshly ground black pepper

1 Egg, beaten

90 gm/3 oz/1½ cups breadcrumbs

2-3 tbsp Oil

Method:

Mix the minced meat and bacon in a bowl. Pound them together well with the back of a mixing spoon. Add the onion, chillies, tomato paste, mustard and mace.

Sprinkle in salt and pepper, and add the egg. Mix the ingredients into the meat until thoroughly combined. Lastly mix in the breadcrumbs. Cover and chill for 30 minutes.

To shape the meatballs, wet your hands. Then take small portions of the mixture and roll them into rounds, keeping your hands wet to prevent the meat from sticking and to make the surface of the meatballs smooth.

Heat the oil in a large frying pan and cook the meatballs, turning them gently, then rolling them as they become firm, until they are browned all over outside and cooked through. Drain on absorbent paper and serve hot or cold.

Mozzarella Toasts

Ingredients:

1 short French stick, cut into 2.5 cm/1 inch slices

1 Garlic clove, crushed and chopped

2 tbsp Olive oil

12 Large Basil leaves, shredded

5 Ripe tomatoes, peeled, deseeded and roughly chopped

Salt and freshly ground black pepper

12 Large Basil leaves, shredded

225 g / 8 oz Mozzarella cheese, thinly sliced

Frech stick, cut into 2.5 cm / 1 inch slices

12 Black (ripe) olives, pitted

12 Small Basil leaves to garnish

Method:

Toast the French bread slices on one side. Mix the garlic with the olive oil and brush a little over the untoasted sides of the bread slices. Top each slice with some Basil shreds and tomato, and season well with salt and pepper. Place a slice of mozzarella on top of each and brush with any remaining oil and garlic.

Cook the toasts under a hot grill (broiler) until bubbling and golden when you are ready to serve them. Top each with an olive and garnish with a Basil leaf. Serve immediately.

Garlic Mushroom Puffs

Ingredients:

125 gm / 4 oz / ½ cup Firm-textured,
low-fat soft cheese (the type sold in
packets, such as Shape cheese)
1 Garlic clove, crushed
2 tbsp Parsley
1 tbsp Snipped chives
3 tbsp Fresh white breadcrumbs
Salt and freshly ground black pepper
18 Closed cap (button) mushrooms, stalks
removed
225 gm / 8 oz Puff pastry, thawed if frozen
1 Egg, beaten, to glaze

Method:

Mix the soft cheese with the garlic, parsley,
chives, breadcrumbs and salt and pepper
to taste. Place a little filling in each of the
mushrooms, pressing it in well to the cavity
left by the stalk.

Roll out the pastry into a 30 cm / 12
inch square and cut it into 5 cm / 2 inch
strips, then across into 5 cm / 2 inch
squares. Sandwich each of the mushrooms
between two pastry squares, brushing
the edge of the pastry with a little beaten
egg to seal in the mushrooms. Place on a
baking sheet and chill for 30 minutes.

Glaze the pastry with the beaten egg and
bake at 220° C / 425° F / gas 7 for about
10 minutes, or until puffed and golden.
Cool on a wire rack.

Buttered Nuts

Ingredients:

125g/4 oz / 1 stick Butter; clarified

1 Bay leaf

450g/1 lb/ 4 cups Shelled, unsalted almonds, pecans, brazils, hazelnuts, walnuts or a mixture of these nuts

1 tsp Coarsely ground sea salt

¼ tsp Paprika

Pinch of cayenne pepper

A little fresh grated nutmeg

Method:

Pour the strained (clarified) butter into a large, heavy bottomed saucepan and add the bay leaf. Cook the bay leaf on its own, pressing it with the back of a mixing spoon, for 1 minute, until it gives off its aroma.

Add the nuts and heat gently. Cook, stirring often, until the nuts are evenly browned but not too dark or they will taste bitter.

Clarified Butter

Melt the butter in a small saucepan over low heat, leave it to cook gently for about 5 minutes, or until a sediment has formed in the bottom of the pan. Take care not to overheat and brown the butter. Meanwhile, line a metal sieve (strainer) with a piece of muslin (cheesecloth) and rest it on a basin; then pour in the butter, discarding the sediment.

Chickpea Crunch

Ingredients:

439g/15 oz can chickpeas

3 tbsps Plain (all purpose) flour

2 tsp Ground cumin

2 tsps Dried oregano

Generous pinch of cayenne pepper

½ tsp Salt

Oil for deep-frying

Method:

Drain the chickpeas in a sieve. Mix the flour, cumin, oregano, cayenne pepper and salt in a bowl. Shake the chickpeas well; then add them to the flour mixture. Use a spoon to toss the chickpeas in the flour mixture until thoroughly coated.

Pour some oil for deep frying into a small pan – the pan should be no more than a quarter full. It is not worth heating a large amount of oil as it cannot be used for frying other foods because it will be flavoured with the flour and spice mixture.

Heat the oil to 190°C/375°F or until a cube of day-old bread browns in about 30 seconds. Add about half the chickpeas (or as many as can be fried in the oil) and cook for about 5 minutes, until crisp and golden. Use a slotted spoon to remove the chickpeas from the oil; then drain them well on double-thick absorbent kitchen paper. Cook the remaining chickpeas. The hot chickpeas can be sprinkled with a little extra salt if liked, while hot.

Allow to cool before serving.

Index

ISBN: 978-81-7436-722-8

© Roli & Janssen BV 2009
Published in India by Roli Books in arrangement with Roli & Janssen BV
M-75, G.K. II Market; New Delhi-110 048, India.
Phone: ++91-11-40682000
Fax: ++91-11-29217185
Email: info@rolibooks.com,
Website: rolibooks.com

Design: Supriya Saran
Layout: Nabanita Das
Production: Naresh Nigam & Rajeev Kumar

Printed and bound in Singapore.